MW00873250

WHY?

✦

AFRICAN AMERICAN CHILDREN CAN NOT READ

Philip Cooper

iUniverse, Inc.
New York   Bloomington

WHY?

AFRICAN AMERICAN CHILDREN CAN NOT READ

Copyright © 2009 by Philip Cooper

All rights reserved. No part of this book may be used or reproduced by any means, graphic, electronic, or mechanical, including photocopying, recording, taping or by any information storage retrieval system without the written permission of the publisher except in the case of brief quotations embodied in critical articles and reviews.

iUniverse books may be ordered through booksellers or by contacting:

iUniverse
1663 Liberty Drive
Bloomington, IN 47403
www.iuniverse.com
1-800-Authors (1-800-288-4677)

Because of the dynamic nature of the Internet, any Web addresses or links contained in this book may have changed since publication and may no longer be valid. The views expressed in this work are solely those of the author and do not necessarily reflect the views of the publisher, and the publisher hereby disclaims any responsibility for them.

ISBN: 978-0-595-45735-9 (pbk)
ISBN: 978-0-595-90036-7 (ebk)

Printed in the United States of America

iUniverse rev. date: 1/7/2009

Now never begins yesterday. To set afoot a new and whole black woman and man, we must first tell the victims what happened to them—before and after America was new.

Randall Robinson, *The Debt*

To Mom and Dad

To my enduring family.
To Roma Witzig, for believing in me.
To Derrick Mahony, for the epiphany of looking beyond the obvious.
To the children whose quality of life will be brighter because of *Why?*

Contents

Preface

In the spring of 1999, I was cruising the television channels and stopped to watch a repeat of a CBS *48 Hours* segment on sleep apnea. The segment followed a seven-year-old boy named Adam. Adam was hyperactive, he did not perform well in school and had been diagnosed with attention deficit disorder. In addition to this diagnosis, his medical history revealed that he snored while sleeping. The nightly episodes of snoring were punctuated with periods of apnea, which is a temporary cessation of breathing, and arousals, which are brief periods of awakening. After doctors performed a sleep study, Adam was diagnosed with a mild form of obstructive sleep apnea. Doctors discovered that his airway was blocked by large adenoids and tonsils. Medical intervention to remove these structures resulted in the elimination of Adam's snoring. The intervention also resulted in a significant change in his behavior pattern and major improvements in his academic progress.

A percentage of my general dental practice is devoted to orthodontics. Historically, orthodontics has focused on corrective protocols, such as straightening "crooked" teeth. Today, however, the focus has shifted to early intervention and prevention. Orthodontists now pay particular attention to the anatomical growth and development of the facial structures that support the teeth. Many factors impact the growth and development of these facial structures, but the primary biological conditions that negatively affect the developmental process are airway obstructions and blockages.

My patient population is predominantly African American, with many children whose medical histories include treatment for asthma, allergies, bronchitis, and hyperactivity The content of the *48 Hours* program stimulated me to ask whether treating the snoring and breathing problems of these children would have similar results.

In this day of increasing disparities, which I will discuss in more detail, African American children often do not receive the same level of attention that many of their counterparts receive in both medical and educational contexts. We will see that it is the intertwining of social, economic, and health care disparities that underpin the negative perception of African American children who struggle in school, behave poorly, and fail to achieve.

My objective is to begin the process of changing the negative perception of African American children in the educational environment and in society as a whole. This is a book about reading and those factors that predispose many African American children to struggle with reading. I want to be very clear: The disproportionate number of African American children who struggle with reading is unacceptable, particularly in a society that has the capacity to educate all of its children. There *is* an answer. If we address the reasons *why* African American children cannot read, we can begin to replace society's pessimistic projections for the fate of African American children with optimism.

Introduction

Not all African American children perform poorly in the educational environment because they struggle with reading and reading comprehension. In fact, many African American children perform equally as well as children of other races and nationalities, and in many instances they excel. However, a disproportionately high percentage of African American children *do struggle* and are less than proficient. These children are the focus of *Why?*

All too often, children who fail to achieve proficiency are classified as at risk even before they begin the formal education process, based purely on the perception of their social and economic status. These children are often classified as "special," "slow learners," "uneducable," "behavior problems," and, in one state system, "other health impaired." These children may not have hearing, vision, or mental deficits, but because they differ from the "norm," they are singled out as needing "special" attention. Why are these children so different from those African American children who become doctors, lawyers, inventors, and productive citizens? The skill exhibited by successful children is the ability to read and comprehend with proficiency.

On April 28, 1998, Dr. G. Reid Lyon, then the government guru of reading at the National Institute of Child Health and Human Development, presented a report to the Senate Committee on Labor and Human Resources in which he made the following statement:

> Consider that reading skill serves as the major avenue
> to learning about other people, about history and

social studies, the language arts, science, mathematics, and other content subjects that must be mastered in school. When children do not learn to read, their general knowledge, their spelling and writing abilities and their vocabulary development suffer in kind. Within this context, reading skill serves as the major foundational skill for all school-based learning, and without it, the chances for academic and occupational success are limited indeed. Because of its importance and visibility, particularly during the primary grades, difficulty learning to read squashes the excitement and love for learning that many youngsters enter school with.

It is significant that Dr. Lyon referred to the preschool years as a critical period in a child's development of the ability to read. He writes,

Some children learn to read and write with ease. Even before they enter school, they have developed an understanding that the letters on a page can be sounded out to make words and some preschool children can even read words correctly that they have never seen before and comprehend what they have read.

The quality of a child's early environment has garnered considerable attention at the local, state, and national levels of education. Current neurological research indicates the importance of the environment in providing the stimulus and exposure necessary for the development of the neural pathways involved in memory and cognition.

The child's socioeconomic status and home environment often mirrors the level of their academic progress, particularly when it, too, is a part of the cycle of poverty, which we will discuss. When race is factored in, the percentage of children, who live in poverty and are considered at risk for poor academic performance, is significantly higher in those regions where the African American population is concentrated. The impact of poverty and other social and economic factors on the quality of academic performance begs the following question: *Which comes first, poor academic performance or low socioeconomic status?*

With the increased emphasis on early childhood development and an expanded knowledge of the process of brain development and its impact on children's readiness for school, education is becoming more involved in the preschool years. More and more state governments are increasing the funding for their pre-kindergarten programs. With the government-backed No Child Left Behind program as the catalyst, many brain-based teaching and learning systems, both commercial and educational, are reporting measurable levels of success. It is ironic that the subliminal message of the United Negro College Fund's battle cry—"the mind is a terrible thing to waste"—is that the quality of the mind and brain will determine the level of success for many children.

The axiom, "one cannot see the forest for the trees", is applicable in the search for the key or keys to academic success. In the 2001 blockbuster movie, *Gladiator*, the opening scene is an epic battle of the Roman Empire's army against a barbarian horde. As the scene fills the screen with thousands of men fighting furiously, there is one standard-bearer for the Roman army who is clearly not involved in the fighting. Instead, he is smiling and looking around, as if he was taking a walk in the park, perhaps, just enjoying the fact that he is in a movie. I am sure the screen editors saw the fault but considered it acceptable because, with so much action happening on the screen barely nine minutes into the movie, viewers would hardly notice this happy-go-lucky actor, notwithstanding the fact that reshooting the scene would have entailed considerable cost.

Too often, educators become involved in the educational process and overlook the fundamental element in the equation, namely, the child. The prevailing assumption has been that all children, with exceptions of course, enter the formal education environment with the neural systems and cognitive skills necessary for developing the ability to read. All educators have to do is find the right technique or method for facilitating the process of learning to read. The cognitive skills in question rely upon the neural systems involved in memory, which are necessary for developing reading skills. *Why?* explores the social, economic, and biological factors that influence the growth and development of this critical neural system and, more specifically, how these factors impact a large percentage of African American children.

Why African American children? The National Center for Educational Statistics (NCES) has consistently presented annual data that identifies the African American male student as the least proficient student in multiple categories of academic achievement, particularly, reading proficiency. The

NCES data demonstrates that the reading levels of fourth- and eighth-graders who read at or above proficient has not changed since Lyon's 1998 report. According to the NCES 2003 *Nation's Report Card*, the percentage of public school students at or above proficient in reading was 30 percent in both the fourth and eight grades, leaving 70 percent reading below proficient. In children from low-income families, the disparity is greater: the percentage below proficient was closer to 85 percent. Contrary to the reported statements from individual states, agencies, and education's highest official, the U.S. Secretary of Education, the data suggest there has been little, if any, significant change in student performance. Over the past 20 years, millions of dollars have been spent on academic programs that specifically target children who struggle in the academic environment. And yet, identifiable populations of children, particularly African American children, continue to struggle with reading proficiency. Why? What have educators and social scientists overlooked?

If you have ever played Connect the Dots, then you will understand the approach of this revealing book, as it connects the historical, social, biological, and educational factors that contribute to the lack of academic proficiency among African American children. It will dispel the notion that children from poor economic backgrounds are inherently inferior to their counterparts in higher economic brackets; and it will dispel the notion that African American children are, somehow, missing certain genetic endowments needed for learning.

The U.S. Department of Education's research efforts have targeted the areas of scientifically based instructional practices that will result in improved academic achievement, particularly, in reading and math. On the other side of the research spectrum, medical science has identified conditions, such as obstructive sleep apnea syndrome (OSAS) that interfere with the growth and development of specific regions and functions of the brain, specifically those functions needed for the development of the memory pathways. The ability to read is a complex neural process that involves synergetic relationships between multiple areas of the brain, including those responsible for vision, hearing, and, most importantly, memory. This book will show how reading skills relate to disparities in health care, socioeconomic status, and education, with emphasis on their impact on this critical developmental process.

The foundation for normal educational advancement is developed long before the child enters the formal education environment. Beginning in the womb, the infant's brain develops in response to stimuli in its environment.

After birth, this process continues as the environment expands and the number and range of stimuli increase. Brain-based educational programs and systems abound, primarily, focusing on the instructional application of the brain's ability for change and modification, called plasticity, in later childhood. However, it is the growth of the brain in infancy, a brain that is in the process of creating its areas of functional specialization, that holds the key to academic success. It would be ideal if educators knew *why* students cannot read; this would allow for the development of instructional modalities that are more applicable and effective.

Change is the law of life, and those who concentrate on the past or the present are certain to miss the future.

John F. Kennedy

Chapter 1

Past Is Present

One cannot discuss education from an African American perspective without reflecting on the impact that social and economic factors, both historical and present, have had on the process of education. As descendants of slaves, African American children have been forced to follow a more complex path toward securing an education than their counterparts. It is not my intent to revisit the history of slavery or to expand the plethora of books and articles written by experts and historians. Those who desire a serious historical analysis of the correlation between slavery and black equality in America may wish to consult one of the many excellent texts, such as Anthony Asadullah Samad's *50 Years after Brown: The State of Black Equality in America* (2005). What is significant about the history of slavery is how forced servitude and the social attitude that perpetuated it are manifested in the social, economic, and educational environments in which we live today.

When the first waves of African slaves were deposited on the shores of Virginia in 1619, not only did their physical landscape change, the cultural fiber of their African heritage began to decay. Centuries of strong social, economic, and family infrastructures were systematically torn apart in the new world, as families were separated and distributed across the new land. Slaves were neither allowed nor encouraged to learn to read or go to school. This was one of the many ways that slave owners attempted to control their "property." Separating families and cross-breeding stripped them of their native language. In its place, slaves were given a new language, a language whose subliminal message was one of servitude to the master. Even after the slaves were freed, few efforts were made to level the playing field. Former slave owners knew and understood that slaves were smart and competent enough to run their plantations, so when the slaves were freed, they hired them on as skilled servants. During the Reconstruction years following the Civil War, these freed men and women, who were the very backbone and fiber of the plantation, were considered intellectually inferior to whites and socially inadequate. This view was a means of continued subjugation of blacks, for otherwise they would have been allowed to compete in society and the work force as equals. The period following the Civil War was notably the greatest period of social oppression for the freed slaves. Using the ruse, "separate but equal," southern whites were able to bolster their efforts to return slaves to a subordinate position. Jim Crow was the Trojan Horse of politics, allowing freed slaves to be systematically managed and controlled within the constraints of legal mumbo-jumbo. The right to work, the right to be educated, and the right to vote—these separated whites from blacks. These were unquestionably the inalienable rights of whites, while blacks struggled and even died trying to exercise the simplest of human rights. From 1609 to 1865, the objective of the Civil Rights Movement was freedom from slavery, and from 1866 to 1964, the objectives were citizenship, voting rights, equal access to public facilities, and school desegregation. Those who wish to de-emphasize the impact of slavery on today's societal ills would do well to heed what Professor Cornel West writes,

> Like every younger generation, our kids today see clearly the hypocrisies and mendacities of our society, and as they grow up they begin to question in fundamental ways some of the lies that they've received from society. They also begin to see that their education has been distorted and sugarcoated and has sidestepped so many uncomfortable truths. (West 2004)

Despite this history of restricted access to education, many slaves and their descendants have made significant contributions in education, science, and industry.

Segregation

Little Rock, Arkansas, "separate but equal," and *Brown v. The Board of Education of Topeka*—what do they have in common? They all refer to events in history that were attempts by the American democratic conscience to address the perpetuation of racial inferiority in the post–Civil War era. After the Civil War, and some say even to this day, people of African descent in America have had to wage a continual battle to gain a measure of equality, a battle with the democratic society that was built upon their backs. Racial segregation of the races was overt in some environments, but it could also be very subversive in others, education included. After the historical Brown decision in 1954, which gave rise to legislation that was supposed to equalize the playing field for blacks in the education arena, educators replaced race with disability as a bench mark of division. Children who did not meet certain performance guidelines or lacked certain testable basic skills were grouped together to address their specific needs. Now, fifty years later, exclusion is the dividing modality used in educational separation. The tools of exclusion are race, disability and (re)segregated education. Since 1954, there has been a lack of progress toward racial integration in schools nationwide, as evidenced by the fact that, statistically, students of color are overrepresented in special education programs. These are programs based on a child's disability. The discourses of racism and ableism that support these programs have bled into one another, permitting forms of racial segregation under the continuing guise of disability.

My daily routine begins with reading the newspaper around five o'clock in the morning. Invariably, there is at least one article that either cites statistical evidence of deficiencies in academic achievement among children at risk or from low-income families, or reports some effort to close the "achievement gap." What does "at risk" really mean? Is it a term used to identify, target, or separate specific groups of children because of their social, economic, biological, or cultural environments? Or is it a means of identifying those children who, without intervention, will likely struggle in the academic environment? The determination of a child's disability and, more importantly, the point in the child's life when that determination is made, are critical to the child's path of progress in the educational process.

Jamal was a four-year-old boy whose mother and father were not married and he was on public assistance. According to his pre-kindergarten teacher, he was struggling with the language skills necessary for future academic growth and development and would not do well in kindergarten This teacher's unconstructive assessment had the potential to initiate the downward spiral for a poor academic achiever. This type of early negative assessment, particularly when it becomes a part of a child's academic record, all too often follows the student throughout his entire academic life and can be used as grounds for disability segregation. The intent of the 1975 Education of All

Handicapped Children Act (P.L. 94.142) was to guarantee disabled students an education in the least restricted environment. This legislation, now the Individuals with Disabilities Education Act (IDEA), is the template for special education programs across the country. Statistically, African American children are over-represented in programs that are based on this practice of disability labeling.

Trisha was an eight-year-old girl in second grade who was performing below grade level in reading and mathematics. She appeared lethargic and inattentive, and the teachers recommended she be placed in the Early Intervention Program (EIP) designed for students considered at risk for failure. As part of her evaluation, her parents were advised of the possibility of using medication to stimulate her performance. Since she lived in a two-parent home, the economic status of which would have been considered middle class, socioeconomic status was not a factor, yet she was being considered for exclusion (segregation) because of her performance level. Some argue that educational testing and evaluation practices are not racially biased; others argue to the contrary. Jamal and Trisha were assessed and considered at risk, yet their socioeconomic conditions were different. The one constant factor for both children was their race; they were African American.

Poverty

Social and educational theorists regard the socioeconomic background of a child as a critical factor in the projected success or failure of that child in the formal education environment. However, the proverbial "Which comes first, the chicken or the egg?" can be applied here. Are children who perform poorly in the educational arena a product of their socioeconomic status, or is their socioeconomic status the product of poor education? Adult literacy is a target of many local, state, and federal programs, often in conjunction with efforts to reduce poverty. Is it not ironic that these illiterate adults were once children entering the first grade, ready and eager to learn?

Poverty has been defined as a culture within itself, with its own set of rules, values, and even language. The lack of education, and particularly the ability to read, is a primary factor in the cycle of poverty. Children in poverty often do not know that they are poor, because their environments are part of a cycle of existence that essentially perpetuates itself. They do not know they are "poor" until someone tells them so or treats them as being "poor." Two terms are commonly used in definitions for poverty: "generational poverty," which refers to families who are in poverty for at least two generations, and "situational poverty," which refers to a condition of poverty that lasts for a shorter period of time and is caused by circumstances, such as death and illness. Perhaps, for African Americans, there should be a third category, "historical poverty," because their very existence in this country was founded in poverty.

Eligibility for free or reduced-price school lunches is an indicator of children in poverty. It is significant that current national reading assessment scores for this group are lower than the average scores for students who were not eligible, and that African American children make up a large percentage of the eligible population. The No Child Left Behind legislation was designed to address the needs of children who are struggling and considered at risk. This legislation has both supporters and detractors. Many of the opinions, on both sides, mirror the views aired in the early days of desegregation, more than fifty years ago. The tools of segregation and division are now exclusion, testing, and socioeconomic classification.

WHY AM I AT RISK?
Is it because my mother is single?
Is it because my father does not live with us?
Is it because I receive free lunches?
Is it because my mother did not finish high school?
Is it because I perform poorly in school?
Is it because I see no future beyond my neighborhood?
Is it because I say screet for street?
Is it because my school is a Title I school?
Is it because someone said I am?
Is it all of the above or none of the above?

Is it more than the above?

Chapter 2

The Brain

The brain is the central processing unit of the body. It controls the motor, sensory, and other functions of the body. The brain has the ability to develop the complex system of nerve cell connections called "memory." The extent and quality of memory serves as the basis for language acquisition and is the database for reading and reading comprehension. In schools across the country, reading assessment data is used to identify children who are struggling and at risk of failure. Children who can sound out words in the earlier grades often fail in the later grades, when comprehension becomes the focus and not simply the technical skill of sounding out words. According to some theorists, reading comprehension is based on knowledge. There is merit to this idea, if one understands that knowledge is synonymous with memory, in the neural sense.

Reading is a fundamental and necessary skill in the educational process. Learning to read, however, is not innate. It is a neurally based skill that is one of the most complex cognitive functions the brain performs, utilizing the centers for vision, hearing, judgment, and, most importantly, memory. Simply defined, memory is the system of neural pathways connecting cells in the brain. With recent advances in neurological research, scientists now know the specific areas of the brain used in processing language and the time frame during which the brain develops the memories required for reading and reading comprehension.

"I Got One" is a game my grandchildren play for word recognition. If the game is about colors, I say, "I got one: blue." Mara, the three-year-old, will laugh and laugh, and then she says, "I got one: red." This goes on and on until she cannot think of another color. At that point, her facial expression reflects a processing mode, as her brain goes down the list of colors, trying to find a color she has not used. Her six-year-old brother is a more advanced player, primarily, because his brain has had more exposure to language and time to develop more memory. They also play the game with fruits, letters, and sounds, but they always reach that point where they exhaust their memory.

How is memory developed, and how do we keep it? At birth, the brain is composed of billions of cells (neurons), some specialized, such as those for vision and hearing, and others called undifferentiated cells, whose functions will be determined by stimulation and need. Neurons become memory when they develop specific permanent connections (axons and dendrites) to surrounding cells. The more axons and dendrites that are connected, the more complex the network, and hence the larger the memory. There are essentially two schools of thought regarding brain development. One is the "open book" theory, in which data and information are received, catalogued, and retained on the blank pages of the book; the more information, the bigger the book. This would seem to be reasonable and logical because the brain grows, physically in proportion, with the rest of the body. On the other hand, some scientists theorize that the brain is "prewired" for various functions, and the nerve cells only need to be stimulated to perform their designated function. Clinical research has presented evidence that each of these theories contains an element of truth and is involved in growth and development.

What is significant is that the brain of nearly every child (with the obvious exceptions of injuries and certain birth defects) possesses the same potential for growth and development. For years, mothers have been encouraged to read, sing, and listen to music during their pregnancy to stimulate the developing fetal brain. After birth, the child's immediate environment is the predominant source of stimulation. Specialized cells begin the process of organizing themselves within the constraints of their specific genetic coding and the undifferentiated cells respond to stimuli. This is a biological process and is subject to change due to variations in the nature of the internal or external stimuli the child encounters. An example is the brain's need for oxygen. The medical emergency condition referred to as "stroke" occurs when there is a blockage or interruption of the supply of oxygen to the brain. The amount of time the brain can do without oxygen before becoming permanently damaged is quite limited, approximately four minutes. Based on purely biological analysis, it is reasonable and logical to conclude that, if the oxygen demands of the developing brain are not sufficiently met during the growth process, there will be a measurable impact on the quality of the final neural connections.

The brains of children between the ages of two and five consume twice as much blood glucose (their principal source of energy) as the brains of adults; this is due in part because their brains are in the business of forming the vast number of neural connections needed for memory and other developing functions. Sufficient amounts of oxygen are required to process the glucose and form the neural cell connections. A common cold is an example of a situation that can impact brain development. The cold causes respiratory congestion; thus, the child does not breathe well and cannot provide his or her body with the optimum levels of oxygen needed for neural cell development. In optimal oxygenation enviroments the brain develops those neural systems necessary for the development of language.

Language

We have all seen people who are one nationality by birth but speak English as their dominant language. Why and how this happens is the direct function of the brain in the acquisition of language. Volumes have been written that describe the brain's role in perception, attention, critical thinking, social behavior, emotion, and language. The time frame for basic language acquisition is believed to end or at least decrease significantly about the age of three. At eleven months, a child's brain can distinguish subtle differences in the phonetic sounds of different languages. But twelve months later, if the child has been exposed to just one language, as is the norm in the United States, the child's ability to detect such differences in another language begins to diminish. Bilingual children, who grow up in a household where both languages are spoken regularly, can shift from one to the other without a discernible accent. Those who learn the second language after this critical time period are far more likely to speak the second language with the accent of the primary language. Failure of the brain to make the neural connections responsible for language leads to speech, reading, and writing difficulties.

A number of brain-based programs and instructional methods are reporting success in helping students make performance gains. Through the understanding of neural-cognitive plasticity, which is the brain's continuing ability to modify or change its physical structure, these brain-based programs are able to enhance the capacity of students to think, learn, and communicate.

The potential for neural-cognitive plasticity, however, is predicated on the fact that the student's brain has developed the basic neural connections that can be modified. There are specific periods in the brain's development that are critical for future language expression. During these particularly sensitive periods, the brain is actively constructing the necessary pathways and needs optimum supplies of oxygen. If there is insufficient oxygen (oxygen deprivation), these networks of pathways may be incomplete or may not develop to their full potential, causing the possibility of cognitive development impairment. Some research indicates that a lack of oxygen (hypoxia) after birth in premature babies places them at a greater risk for future cognitive and language problems, proportionate to the degree of hypoxia (Hopkins-Golightly et al. 2003). Similarly, the child who suffers from sleep apnea will lack a significant amount of REM sleep and will have low levels of oxygen in the blood, both of which can have lasting effects on the developing brain.

Altered or restricted breathing conditions lower the amount of oxygen available for use by the brain cells. As noted above, upper airway obstructions are a prime causative factor in sleep apnea and are also associated with musculoskeletal dysfunction of the head and neck. Of particular interest to educators is the impact of such dysfunctions on the ear, tongue, and muscles of speech. Eustachian tube dysfunction and conductive hearing loss are associated with the enlargement of structures in the pharynx, the adenoids, and tonsils, anatomically located just medial to the inner portion of the ear. Children who cannot properly hear the sounds of letters will not be able to reproduce those sounds in reading and speaking. A large percentage of students whom teachers identify as struggling are the students who always have their mouths open, look sleepy, or fall asleep in class. This mouth-open posture is called "mouth breathing" and is an abnormal function adopted when children with obstructive sleep apnea syndrome (OSAS) cannot breathe through their nose. The muscles of the jaw realign themselves to accommodate the need for air, resulting in irregular tongue posture and vaulted palates (V-shaped roof of mouth). These musculoskeletal changes also affect speech patterns and compromise phonetic sound production, resulting in children being assigned to speech therapy classes because they do not meet phonetic proficiency.

Poor speech ability is sometimes the result of ankyloglossia, or tied tongue. This condition usually presents itself when the tip of the tongue is attached to the floor of the mouth and cannot perform the movements necessary for those sounds that require the tip to make full contact with the anterior palate (e.g., the initial sounds in lake, like, lucky, and love). For other students, producing the phonetic sounds of language is difficult because of inadequate muscle function that accompanies their malpositioned jaw. Speech therapists trained in myofunctional therapy focus on training or retraining the muscles used for phonetics and sound production. Poor language skills have been implicated as contributing to a person's difficulty in sustaining social relationships, making moral decisions, and controlling anger and other emotions.

Though there have been great advances in understanding brain development, there is still much to be learned about how to improve and protect the development of the brain. Of the many brain-based teaching programs that I reviewed in the preparation of this text, such as Dr. Robert Titzer's Your Baby Can Read and Ruby Payne's "Aha" Process, most were found to be *method-mode* forms of instruction. The method mode understands the brain's development and provides applicable strategies and modalities for improvement. The "read aloud" method, for example, assumes that if the child can read words fluently and accurately out loud, then reading skills will follow naturally, given exposure and a wider range of reading experiences, such as having more books in the home, being read to, and so forth. What has been demonstrated is that enhanced general knowledge and vocabulary result from such exposure, but do not guarantee a comprehensive reader. Children who can sound out words fluently and accurately but cannot successfully understand much of what they have read will not benefit from wide reading. Special reading programs, curriculum adjustments, and other educational innovations have produced little, if any, statistical improvement in the reading abilities of specific populations of children, including African American children. For educators, the idea is that the implementation of the right method will help the right child to improve. We now understand that improving the cognitive skills of sub-proficient children will have more impact in closing the proverbial education gap.

A healthy brain needs a healthy body to supply the essential elements for optimum function. When a child is not healthy, the body and brain are not at their most efficient level of productivity. A child's level of health is critical for day-to-day activity and even more so for their growth and development, especially between the ages of two and five.

Chapter 3

Health Care Disparity

From the Trauma Unit in the Emergency Room to the office of the Primary Care Physician (PCP), the mission of health care providers—physicians, nurses, and physician's assistants—is to provide quality medical care for all patients. Due to the rising cost of malpractice insurance, the risk of litigation and restricted budgets, providers often feel they are in a sea of emotions that directly affect their choice of diagnostic and treatment modalities. The issue of health care disparity for African Americans and other minorities is chronicled in study after study and research project after research project. For our purposes, disparity in health care exists whenever the health status of a population subgroup—defined by demographic factors such as gender, age, race, ethnicity, socioeconomic status, level of education, geographic location, disability, or sexual orientation—is significantly lower than that of other groups.

It is 6:30 p.m. in the Emergency Room (ER) of the local hospital. Jerome, a four-year-old African American male, sits in his mother's lap. He is wheezing and having difficulty breathing, waiting for the nurse to call him. This will be the fourth time this year that Jerome's mother has brought him to the ER with the same problems. Eventually, the nurse calls his name, and he is seen by the doctor and treated for his wheezing. He leaves feeling better. His mother receives a couple of prescriptions and instructions to administer breathing treatments when necessary. Jerome's medical history includes a diagnosis of asthma complicated by bronchitis. The home treatment for acute asthmatic episodes is the application of medications using a Nebulizer, a system that creates a mist the patient inhales via a facial mask. Jerome was prescribed a Nebulizer a year prior to this current episode, and the medications prescribed duplicate those he received the last three times he was treated in the ER, and by his PCP during normal office visits. It should be noted that Jerome has been treated in his PCP's office multiple times for the same condition within the same time period of his ER visits. Today's experience in the ER seems routine on the surface, but a broader look at his situation reveals a more complex set of circumstances and factors in play. Jerome was in the ER because his mother called his PCP that morning and was unable to get an appointment. This is a familiar occurrence in the offices of providers who participate in public-assisted health care programs, because Schedules are often double and triple booked to accommodate the volume of patients and to compensate for patients who miss appointments, something that is common among program enrollees.

Then there is the issue of reimbursement. Payments to providers for services rendered are often low, slow to arrive, and many times lost in the struggle to meet program budgets. The number of providers in these programs has fluctuated over the years, with many doctors refusing to accept public assistance patients because of these unpredictable conditions. In many rural areas, the situation is exacerbated by an extreme shortage of providers. Many small county hospitals have all but closed their doors while waiting on payments from state agencies for services rendered. This situation is compounded when these facilities provide services to indigent patients who have no health coverage and no means to pay; all of these circumstances are factors in the formula for disparity in the delivery of services. Physicians are similarly restricted, by program codes, as to what services they can and cannot provide, therefore visits are confined to the most expedient assessment, diagnosis, and treatment scenario possible. This is not to say that providers do not care about their patients, but these factors tend to alter the scope of their diagnostic and treatment modalities. Just as the hospital is a business, so is the physician's office. The doctor has overhead expenses, malpractice insurance, and employee salaries. In other words, doctors need to be reimbursed to survive.

Disparity occurs when there is a lack of a definitive diagnosis in a specific population that historically presents itself with the same signs and symptoms.

At a recent presentation for medical personnel hosted by a large asthma drug manufacturer, an ER physician in attendance stated in a sidebar conversation that he treats the same children "over and over" for acute upper respiratory problems and that they were predominately African American and received public assistance. The manufacturer's representative/presenter was a physician whose practice was associated with a medical school and hospital and whose patient population mirrored the ER physician's in terms of racial makeup and a high rate of multiple visits for acute respiratory conditions.

Jerome is home for now, but in all probability, he will be back in the ER in about three months. A definitive diagnosis for Jerome's condition would have to incorporate at least two additional clinical manifestations: his hyperactivity and snoring at night. When he is not sick, Jerome is a very active kid who is up early and on the go all day. Sometimes his mother has difficulty slowing him down because he is so energized. At the day-care center, he is considered hyperactive and demands a lot of attention; the staff has suggested that he may need medication to slow him down. At nap time, the sounds coming from the three- and four-year-olds range from quiet purring to the loud rumbling of those who snore. Jerome snores louder than most of the other children, and sometimes the sound stops, as if he is trying to catch his breath.

Both snoring and the momentary interruption of breathing are red flags that indicate the existence of sleep-disordered breathing (SDB) conditions such as sleep apnea (SA), obstructive sleep apnea (OSA), or obstructive sleep apnea syndrome (OSAS). Based on clinical studies, SDBs are not specific to race, gender, age, or social status, though they may occur in families or across generations because of repetitive environmental influences. Children whose snoring patterns resemble those of adults are regarded as having OSAS. Does your child snore? And does your child stop breathing at night? These pivotal questions should be asked during the diagnostic examination, because snoring and apnea episodes are primary symptoms that distinguish OSAS from other generic upper-respiratory conditions.

The clinical guidelines established by the American Academy of Pediatrics in 2002 are very specific for children who snore and have reported histories of apnea episodes. It should be noted, however, that these are guidelines and not standards of care, which means the health care provider is not bound by the suggested protocols for diagnosis and treatment and has a reasonable amount of discretion in his or her diagnostic protocol. It is this window of discretion, unfortunately, that precipitates the frequent failure to diagnose OSAS. Some studies (such as Chervin et al. 2001)have shown that pediatric offices and clinics alike rarely ask whether the child snores, nor do they always follow the pediatric guidelines for diagnostic elimination of OSAS, even when the response is positive. This is especially true when the chief complaints also happen to be characteristic of asthma or bronchitis.

The incidence of asthma has reached epidemic proportions and is the focus of numerous studies and initiatives. If we analyze the epidemiological data of asthma (Asthma and Allergy Foundation, **Disparities in Asthma Care** 2003) we find that the African American children who live in poverty represent a large percentage of the children whose health status have diminished or is stagnant. Demographically, the states with the greatest increases of reported asthma and bronchitis cases are, for the most part, the states with high concentrations of African American children: Georgia, Florida, Alabama, Mississippi, North and South Carolina, Tennessee, Virginia, and Louisiana. If you overlay topographical maps, each representing concentrations of people suffering from a particular problem—such as high poverty, elevated number of ADD/ADHD children, large numbers of children with sub-proficient academic performance, and high dropout rates—they would mirror the African American population concentration.

Is there a correlation between race, health care, and education? The answer is yes. Are children in poverty treated differently in the health care arena? The answer is yes. Just as we have seen in education, the perception that certain types of children from certain types of homes and socioeconomic environments are "special" and should be treated differently is also reflected in the medical community. This is not to say that the medical community as a whole is racially prejudiced towards these children, because many of the children in the disparity data are not children of color. There are more White, Hispanic, and mixed-race children living in poverty and receiving public assistance than there are African American children. The glaring disparity is the inordinately high percentage of African American children who are being diagnosed and treated for asthma and bronchitis and not for one of the SDBs. One study (Stepanski et al. 1999) found that African American children with SDB conditions had more arousals (measured by EEG) and greater oxygen desaturation compared to Caucasian and Latino children. This study supported an early study (Redline et al. 1997) which suggested that African American youth may be at increased risk for sleep apnea. The relevance of this data is found in a later study (Chervin et al. 2003), which determined that SDB symptoms are associated with low socioeconomic status and poor school performance.

Of the various breathing disorders, the influence of OSAS and OSA on the growth and development of children is a new frontier and presents a challenge to the academic and medical communities alike. Because clinical symptoms are similar to those of asthma, bronchitis, and upper-respiratory conditions, the initial diagnosis of OSAS and OSA requires the application of secondary and sometimes tertiary diagnostic protocols. The definitive diagnosis for OSA/OSAS includes an examination by an Otolaryngologist (an ear, nose, and throat specialist) and a sleep study to determine the frequency and severity of the apnea. In addition, special x-rays and diagnostic equipment are needed, all of which must be obtained through the referral system. The referral process within the public assistance programs, however, can be an arduous endeavor for the primary care physician and involves coding and budgetary restraints. In their defense, most practitioners cannot afford the time required for the referral process, nor do they have the diagnostic equipment necessary for a secondary level of evaluation, such as cephalometric x-rays, acoustic pharyngometers, and acoustic rhinometers.

As previously indicated, following the guidelines in the initial examination protocol of children who snore would enhance the opportunity for diagnosis at the primary level. In the education arena, the signs and symptoms of SDBs are hyperactivity, short attention span, mouth breathing, poor phonic development, snoring, and overall lack of academic advancement.

Sleep Apnea

Sleep apnea is a life-threatening condition that occurs when breathing stops for a few seconds or longer during sleep. The frequency of apnea episodes determines the severity of the condition. The role of sleep apnea in sudden infant death syndrome (SIDS) has also garnered considerable attention for African American children. According to the National Sudden Infant Death Resource Center, the infant mortality rate for African American children was 2.4 times that of non-Hispanic whites and 2.2 times the SIDS mortality rate of the same population. The direct relationship between sleep apnea and SIDS has not been substantiated by clinical research, but the implications are sufficient to warrant continued serious investigative efforts.

Orthodontists have long understood the adverse effects of sleep-related breathing disorders, specifically OSA, on the growth and development of the face and related dental structures. Habitual mouth breathing is a clinical sign of OSA. It causes the muscles of the face to alter the normal growth pattern of the dental arches and precipitates the development of malocclusions (crooked teeth). Habitual mouth breathing, when combined with conductive hearing loss, results in poor speech and language patterns. Have you ever called a child multiple times and felt that he was just ignoring you and did not respond until you looked him square in the face? The child may have had conductive hearing loss, which occurs when the structures of the throat, the adenoids in particular, are large and put pressure on the inner ear. Mouth breathing restricts the development and alters the shape of the maxilla and mandible (the upper and lower bones of the face). The normal palate is relatively flat and wide, but in mouth breathers, the shape is narrow and often high vaulted, shaped like an inverted V. Phonetic sounds in language are produced when the tongue occludes or touches the palate or roof of the mouth. High vaulted palates, however, limit the tongue's ability to produce many of these sounds, because it cannot reach the palate. The problem is exacerbated if combined with ankyloglossia (tied tongue). When the tip of the tongue remains attached to the floor of the mouth, phonic patterns are distorted and require special attention. Children who are mouth breathers tend to tilt their heads backwards to establish better nasal breathing; altering the position of the cranium affects spinal cord alignment as well as the support systems of the shoulder, pelvis, and feet. OSAS in children has a wide range of clinical signs and must be distinguished from other conditions that have a similar range of signs. Physicians and other health care providers are afforded a measure of discretion in diagnostic and treatment modalities. It is in this area of discretion that the potential for disparity in diagnosing sleep-related breathing disorders lies.

The U.S. Department of Health and Human Services developed the Office of Minority Health to monitor the status of health care for minorities. Jerome's medical condition is chronic in nature and an example of a cycle of disparity that not only diminishes the health status of those not diagnosed but also drives up the cost of health care. The cost of health care increases exponentially each year, with Medicaid as a major contributor. State and federal health budgets are continuously strained; services have to be reduced and often eliminated in the effort to remain within those budgets. In some instances, states run out of money in mid-year and must rely on special legislation to keep up the pace. The pattern of Emergency Room use in Jerome's case is a prime example of a cost driver prevalent among children who receive public assistance health care. Medicaid would be the funding source for Jerome's ER visit charges, the physician's fee for services, and the prescriptions he takes home. When given these parameters of expenditures, multiplied by the number of years he may require treatment, times the number of children treated in the same circumstances, it is easy to see the tremendous effect this scenario can have on health care budgets.

Three of the major cost drivers for the Department of Community Service (under which Medicaid falls) in the state of Georgia for the past four years were (1) Emergency Room visits, (2) treatments for upper-respiratory infections (asthma, bronchitis, etc.), and (3) prescriptions for post-ER treatment (Department of Community Health Reports, 2003–2007). If this sounds familiar, just think of Jerome. The surgical treatment of OSAS would cost approximately three thousand dollars, compared to the approximately two thousand dollar yearly payments for 12 to 14 years of continuous treatment. From 1999 through 2001, the annual prescription drug cost for children with special needs exceeded $13 million, with an average of $530 per child (Ireys, Shulman, and Peterson 2006). Under contract with the Health Resources and Services Administration of the U.S. Department of Health and Human Physical Disability, this study found that illnesses such as asthma, diabetes, and attention deficit disorder were the more common conditions, and prescriptions for these conditions made up more than 70 percent of every dollar spent for 12 percent of the population studied.

Depending upon the severity of the obstruction in OSAS, treatment modalities may include antibiotic therapy and surgical intervention. The removal of an airway obstruction by tonsillectomy or adenoidectomy, and possibly both, would reduce the number of long-term treatment scenarios we have discussed and would reduce the cost of health care. The costs of disparity are measured not only in dollars and cents but also in terms of the effects they have on the quality of life for children, particularly those who are constantly sick and on medication, and on their academic growth and development. Children surgically treated for SDB and OSAS have shown marked improvement in quality of life (Mitchell et al. 2004). Jamal, the child who was expected to struggle in kindergarten because he did not communicate well and did not show good indicators of readiness, was diagnosed and surgically treated for OSAS. His post-treatment academic performance has been exceptional, and he has adjusted socially as well.

As an African American health care provider who for more than 25 years has served a population considered poor, at risk, and socially and economically deprived, I understand the underpinnings of disparity as a fact of life. It is this day-to-day witnessing of disparity and its effects that prompted me to write this book.

In the spring of 2002, I instructed the mother of a ten-year-old child to have the primary care physician (PCP) call me the next time the child had a medical visit. My intent was to alert the PCP that the child had a breathing problem and needed to be referred to a specialist for further evaluation. I chose to speak with the PCP only because the child's next medical visit was a few days away; normally, I would send a narrative report and diagnostic x-rays to support the PCP's referral. (Under Georgia Medicaid guidelines, only the PCP can refer to a specialist.) The PCP did call, and the following is a summary of that conversation.

PCP: Hello, this is Dr. R———. You asked the mother to have me call you when they came in for this visit.

ME: Yes, based on my examination, I strongly suspect that the child has breathing and sleeping problems associated with obstructive sleep apnea.

PCP: We have treated this patient for asthma and bronchitis and believe this is the best course of treatment at his time.

ME: The child has a history of snoring … [PCP interrupting]

PCP: The child is somewhat hyperactive and is having difficulty in school.

The conversation continued for a few minutes and concluded with:

PCP: We will continue to treat the respiratory problem. Thank you for your concern. *Click.*

The child in question was receiving public assistance, lived in a poor section of the county, was considered at risk, and performed poorly in school. Her medical history included snoring, mouth breathing, and chronic nasal and respiratory congestion, and her diagnostic x-rays indicated severe narrowing of her airway passages. The child, who was white, is an example of disparity in health care delivery based on socioeconomic status. Sleep-related breathing disorders such as obstructive sleep apnea occur in all populations.

The PCP in this case refused to accept the possibility that his diagnosis was incorrect and maintained his position despite the signs and symptoms that exceeded those of asthma and bronchitis. It should be noted that this PCP's office was in a rural county where there was a shortage of physicians, and in all probability, it was an extremely busy office, with a large patient base receiving public assistance. It is this type of indifference and lack of definitive diagnosis that impacts the quality of life for many children whose low socioeconomic status is a part of their profile. The cycle of poverty contributing to poor health and poor health contributing to poverty perpetuates the "gap" in both health care and education.

Chapter 4

The Gap

For educators, the achievement gap is defined as the distance between the average score of one group of students compared to that of another group on any given test. The National Center for Education Statistics (NCES), located within the U.S. Department of Education and the Institute of Education Sciences, is the primary federal entity for collecting and analyzing data related to education. In 2005, the NCES reported that the reading performance levels of fourth-grade students showed improvement nationally. However, when the data is filtered to compare the performance levels of African American children to their white counterparts, twice as many African American fourth-graders performed below proficiency. The report also compared student performance on state-generated assessment tools with the National Assessment of Educational Progress (NAEP) test, the assessment tool of the NCES. The results showed that students who performed proficiently on state tests did not maintain that level on the NAEP. Many have criticized the performance mandates of No Child Left Behind (NCLB) and questioned whether states, in the process of restructuring their curriculums and assessment tools to meet these mandates, are in effect reducing their performance criteria for students (i.e., allowing more students to pass in order to show annual yearly progress). Currently, states develop their own tests and assessment tools which allows for varying degrees of structure and measurable content. Many educators feel the standardization of testing and assessment instruments would provide a more accurate comparison of the status of students' reading proficiency collectively. Standardized data could be filtered to further clarify the existence of the differences (gaps) in the performance levels among specific groups of children, such as those students identified as living in poverty.

Which is the precursor of the other, poverty or poor academic achievement? The water is further muddied, because children from both sides of the equation have become exceptionally successful and tremendous contributors to our society. What is so different about these children, and why do they succeed when others do not? Many successful African Americans, like other successful minorities, have stated that they did not know they were "at risk," poor, or disadvantaged until they were older and looked back at their childhood. This leads one to surmise that, perhaps, self-fulfilling prophecies are to blame as the major contributing factor to the gap. How many times do you have to tell a child that he will not make it before he begins to believe it? A middle-school teacher attended an advanced instructional session in which the presenter stated that boys do not like to read. The teacher was somewhat confused, because her two sons, five and nine years of age, were avid readers and loved the intellectual exercise. At home they were required to read a book every night, were only permitted to watch TV for one and a half hours per day, visited the library every weekend, and played video and electronic games only at mom's discretion. This is an example of parental involvement that would be considered the exception in this day of electronic infusion. Children spend more time operating their PlayStations and videogames than doing their homework.

If the instructional experts perpetuate the negative concept of the male student's interest in reading, teachers are likely to enter the classroom with a biased perception of boys' reading interest. A defendant testifies in court that he stole a red car, but the judge instructs the jury to disregard the incriminating statement and to make their judgment based purely on the merits of the case. How do the members of the jury disregard what they have heard? Similarly, how does the teacher, who has been prompted and trained by the experts, enter the classroom without a preconceived notion of her male students' attitude toward reading? The steady stream of statistical reports identifying sub-proficient students as children from backgrounds of poverty has as much to do with the perception and attitude of the teacher entering the classroom as the true abilities of the children themselves.

Simply put, the problems in education and health care are woven from the same fiber. Disparity in education, like disparity in health care, exists whenever the educational status of a population subgroup—defined by demographic factors such as gender, age, race, ethnicity, socioeconomic status, level of education, geographic location, disability, or sexual orientation—is significantly lower than that of other groups.

Dr. Ruby K. Payne is considered by many to be a leading expert in the understanding and teaching of children in poverty. Yet what she suggests is considered a classic example of deficit thinking (Bomer et al. 2008), for she suggests that teachers need to help students who live in less symbol-based home environments learn to process information in the ways formal education demands. To that extent, teachers must recognize that children from poor families often benefit from explicit instruction and support in areas that could be taken for granted among middle-class students. These instructions include the so-called unspoken rules, the mental models that help learners store symbolic information, and the procedures required to complete an abstract task. Dr. Payne also speaks of "poverty's intersection with race." Does this mean that children in poverty are of a certain "race" and are destined to be poor academic performers? If you are an African American reading these words, your heart should be pounding, as you hold your breath and try not to shout "racism." Just as teachers can be programmed to think boys have a low level of interest in reading, they can also have their perception of children in poverty tainted. It would suffice to say that the prejudices, real or imagined, in education toward children in poverty severely undermine the efforts of the well intended. Dr. Payne's, "aha! Process" as well as Marcus Conyers and Donna Wilson's "BrainSMART" and similar programs have claimed some significant changes in some populations. However, the yearly collected national data does not reflect a significant change in poverty levels or academic achievement. Across the board; African American males remain at the bottom of the academic totem pole. Can one assume that these programs are not applicable for children of color? Some educational scholars have taken Dr. Payne to task for stereotyping the poor and consider her work and concepts controversial and based on statistical data rather than clinical research (Boomer et al. 2008).

The introduction of brain-based programs and the restructuring of instructional programs are only the tip of the iceberg when it comes to reducing the educational gap. Reasonable and logical solutions to the educational management of children from poverty tend to address the symptoms but not the root causes of poverty and poor performance. Instructional programs that are designed to assist children from poor backgrounds based on their preconceived deficiencies, genetic, social, or economic status only serve to magnify the elements of ableism and perpetuate the gap.

Ableism

Ableism is a term widely used in disability studies to refer to discrimination and social marginalization resulting from mainstream or majority notions of "ability" that are pervasively projected, in blunt or subtle ways, upon those deemed "disabled." Remember Jamal? His exiting Pre-K assessment was negative, predicting that he would have difficulty in kindergarten. A comprehensive medical exam presented evidence of OSAS, for which medical intervention was recommended. One year after his adenoids and tonsils were surgically removed, his kindergarten progress report indicated he was on track for the first grade. Trisha, who had appeared lethargic and inattentive in class, was considered for placement in an early intervention class; evaluated for behavior modification medication was also diagnosed and treated for OSAS. Her post-surgical schoolwork improved, and she began to perform academically on grade level; she continues to have difficulty with cognitive reading and math skills, due in part to the belated diagnosis and treatment of her OSAS. Both children were struggling in the academic environment because their cognitive skills were impaired by OSAS. Once diagnosed and treated, they were able to get on track and make acceptable progress. They were African American children who were assessed as "at risk" very early in the educational process but were able to advance because their restricting medical conditions were corrected. The potential number of "at risk" children like Jamal and Trisha who's academic progress has been delayed or stifled is staggering.

To say that race and poverty play an integral part in ableism would be an understatement. As we have seen, race and poverty levels have always been considered during the evaluation of African American children. If teachers are instructed, in programs like Ruby Payne's aha! Process, to believe that "poverty" is a direct precipitant of language delays, then the perception is the reality, and the large percentage of African American children who are statistically in "poverty" are truly "at risk" for failure. So where does the gap begin?

Day Care

Each day, thousands of children are dropped off at day-care centers. These centers range from one or two children to fifty or more, depending on the funding sources. These centers, state funded or mom-and-pop operations, are the child's first encounter with formal education, second only to the home environment. Children are exposed to the Alphabet, colors, words, and other stimuli that will help them develop the cognitive skills necessary for the remainder of their lives. As in the case of children like Jamal, the assessment process for school readiness begins in these centers of early learning and have a significant impact on a child's future quality of life. Gene Carter, executive director of the Association for Supervision and Curriculum, has articulated the urgent need for quality early childhood instruction and exposure,

> Over the past several years, "day-care centers" have been popping up almost on every corner. Fueled by the monetary incentives of federal and state dollars, these centers range from in-home mom-and-pop centers to sophisticated and well-funded preschool settings.

So, welcome to Kids World, a preschool facility where the majority of the children come from poor and "at risk" socioeconomic backgrounds. The staff consists of individuals called "child care providers" (CCPs). Their education and instructional backgrounds are varied, ranging from those who have formal early childhood training to those who volunteer their time because they care. The children's ages range from three to five years. The CCPs have the first opportunity to observe, evaluate, and determine the level of academic readiness of these children. They can tell which child is a morning person and which one needs a little more time to get it in gear. Several miles across town is the government-funded Head Start center. The Head Start Program was instituted in the early 1970s to provide "at risk" children with a stimulating social environment that was severely lacking in the home environment. Like their counterparts at Kids World, the CCPs at Head Start know their children and can identify which child has problems with certain sounds or is moody, hyperactive, and so forth. The Head Start Program has come under fire, as some government officials want to scrap the program, stating that it has not produced the level and quality of school preparedness intended.

Now consider the privately funded facilities that are supported by churches, foundations, corporations, and other private entities. The CCPs in the private centers are regarded as better prepared and better trained than the other two centers. It should be noted that the population of the private center is normally less diverse, socially and economically, than the publicly funded centers.

Given these parameters, which group of children would you expect to be best prepared for first grade? A longitudinal study by the Andrew Young School of Policy Studies at Georgia State University compared the progress of children in centers within Georgia as part of a ten-year study. The study concluded that children from the private day-care centers were better prepared when they entered first grade; however, by the end of the first grade, there was no significant difference in the overall performance levels of the children from either type of center. The report's data also reflected a significant decline in the performance levels of African American children after the summer break (Henry, Henderson, and Ponder 2004).

The well-discussed and documented gap between African American and Caucasian children in the formal education environment mirrors the gaps in health care delivery, economic equality, and social status that exist in our society. Despite and perhaps because of No Child Left Behind, funding disparities between high- and low-poverty school systems are worsening; rich systems with lower percentages of low-income children are rewarded with larger federal aid packages, while poor systems with high percentages of low-income children get less. Some states received as much as 51 percent more Title I aid per child than their poorer counterparts. This inequality in funding is another example of the disparities that fuel the perpetuation of the gap. Paralleling these inequalities in education are the well-documented and discussed disparities in health care.

Chapter 5

Obstructive sleep apnea syndrome and other sleep-related breathing disorders have been identified as conditions that impair brain development and subsequently lead to poor academic performance in children.

Obstructive Sleep Apnea Syndrome

Assessing the impact of OSAS and other related conditions on children is a relatively new frontier, for medical professionals and educators alike. As a general dentist who has been in practice for more than 25 years, I thought that I had contributed significantly in providing quality health care. But when I ventured into the world of Orthodontics in 1999, I discovered, to my chagrin, that I was overlooking critical and important factors that impacted my young patients' growth and development. Dentists are the gatekeepers of health. Their medical specialty encompasses the oral cavity, the bones and muscles of the face, and the entrances to the respiratory system, where many medical conditions manifest themselves in the oral cavity. The air that enters the respiratory system through the mouth and nasal passages contains not only viruses but also germs, and microscopic parasites. Irritants also enter the body through the nasal and oral passages and have direct effects on the functions of the digestive, respiratory, and nervous systems, as anyone who has allergies can attest.

The upper portion of the respiratory system is designed to filter the air and remove unwanted particles, and it does so with a reasonable degree of efficiency. The adenoids and tonsils of the throat, along with the nasal cochlea, turbinate, and nasal hairs in the nose, are the primary filters. The ideal respiratory system is a quiet, involuntary system: air passes through the nose, is filtered, and provides the supply of oxygen needed for bodily functions. But when the nose or throat is obstructed by the enlargement of anatomical structures, breathing becomes more difficult and this normally quiet system becomes noisy, as air must be forced through a restricted space.

To compensate for the reduction in airflow caused by nasal and pharyngeal restrictions, the body reverts to mouth breathing. Mouth breathing is not as efficient as nasal breathing, nor is it as healthy. Because the air inhaled through the mouth is not filtered, mouth breathing allows the ingestion of higher levels of unwanted particles and potential irritants. Mouth breathers have noticeably noisy or labored breathing patterns, often associated with obesity; we all know someone who breathes so hard they can be heard from across the room. Then there are those who snore, making noises that sound like a loud rumble in the jungle or a freight train. In adults, snoring and associated sleep apnea have been linked to lost work hours, work-related accidents, and some medical conditions. Snoring in children presents a different set of clinical parameters and conditions that impact the child's growth and development.

The U.S. Department of Education has provided funding for science-based research that will lead to practical classroom methods for improving the achievement levels of students. Advances in medical and biological research are painting a broader picture of the role of science in academic performance. In 1998, Dr. David Gozal of Tulane University evaluated 297 low-performing first-grade students in the New Orleans school system, looking for the presence of snoring and OSAS. The parents of those children diagnosed with OSAS were given the option of surgical intervention (removal of the child's adenoids or tonsils) to correct the obstructed airway condition. Students whose parents elected to allow the intervention improved in their academic performance; those who did not have the intervention continued to struggle academically.

Asthma and ADD/ADHD

The number of children diagnosed with asthma, attention deficit disorder (ADD), or attention deficit hyperactivity disorder (ADHD), all of which have symptoms that mimic those of OSAS, is increasing exponentially. Asthma is a respiratory disorder that causes millions of people to carry inhalers and take medications to control their breathing. According to the nation's watchdog on health issues, the Centers for Disease Control and Prevention (CDC), the number of children diagnosed with asthma is reaching epidemic proportions. Similar increases have been noted in children diagnosed with ADD and ADHD.

Far too often, the recommendation for behavior modification is initiated in schools. Children who are hyperactive, disruptive, inattentive, and lack focus are often assessed for behavior modification. The assessment process is structured to protect the interest of the child and involves the child's parents, teachers, and counselors. This is a critical process, because the child's record may contain a negative assessment that will haunt the student for the remainder of his or her academic life. The primary treatment for ADD is to prescribe medication for behavior control. What concerns me, and many others, is whether a five-year-old placed on medications will ever reach a point when he or she no longer need the medication. "Drug Free School" signs are located on school campuses across the country to indicate that no drugs are tolerated on school property. These signs are oxymorons, because in many schools, the school nurse has more drugs on her shelves, all legal of course, than many small pharmacies.

While preparing to write this book, I attended several presentations by academic and medical experts on child psychology. At one session, I asked the following question: If a five-year-old was referred to you because of a history of hyperactivity, would you medicate first or evaluate the child's total situation? The response was shocking: "I would medicate first," the presenter replied. It should be noted here that the majority of behavior medications are not recommended for children under six years of age because manufacturers lack clinical data to support usage under the age of six.

In a 2002 study, Dr. Ronald Chervin and others evaluated the associations between behavior and sleep-related symptoms by age and sex. He states,

> Children who are sleepy may be more likely to shift their attention frequently and create stimulation to keep themselves awake, especially at young ages when wakefulness is essential to rapid learning.

This statement, when applied to the evaluation process of the problem child in schools, has far-reaching implications. Chervin goes on to state,

In children, experimental sleep deprivation impairs cognitive function, and elementary school children with SDB achieve low grades that improve when the SDB is treated. Cognitive changes associated with untreated SDB may produce inattentive and hyperactive behavior.

Do the children who are being diagnosed and treated as behavioral problems really have ADD or ADHD, or are they just sleepy?

OSAS in Children 3–5 Years Old

Smiles Are Meaningful (SAM) is a nonprofit research organization whose initial focus was the identification of abnormal facial growth and development conditions in African American children who presented with signs and symptoms of OSAS and the associated air exchange problems of sleep apnea, snoring, and asthma. Data reflecting the prevalence of OSAS in children, specifically African American children, was limited and virtually nonexistent. Beginning in 1999, SAM evaluated more than two hundred predominately African American children, three to five years of age, using a protocol of oral examinations, cephalometric x-rays, and medical histories to determine the presence or absence of OSAS. Of those evaluated, 45–50 percent presented with significant signs and symptoms of OSAS, some form of respiratory illness, and sometimes both. Young, Peppard, and Gottlieb (2002) suggested that 14 percent of the population at risk will have OSAS and 1 percent will have obstructive sleep apnea. The children evaluated were enrolled in a local Head Start program of which African American children comprised 98 percent of the population. When one considers the position that African American children maintain in quantitative educational statistics, and the impact OSAS has on children's neurological growth and development, this potentially high percentage of OSAS incidence is significant. This rate of occurrence also mirrors the percentage of African American children who, year after year, struggle in the education process. Previous studies have shown that children who had OSAS showed academic improvement after their conditions were assessed and treated (Gozal 1998).

Another study concluded that impairment in cognition, behavior, and academic performance was exhibited in children with obstructive sleep apnea (Glaze et al. 2002). Of interest to the SAM project was that the incidence of OSAS in children peaks between the ages of two and six (Glaze et al. 2002). This peak period closely parallels the "sensitive period" in the brain's development. Picture a five-year-old with cold or flu symptoms: his or her mouth is open, and breathing is a problem. Now imagine this condition persisting over a six-month period: you have one sick child whose brain is not receiving the levels of oxygen it needs to grow and develop. The medications used to treat ADD/ADHD are either stimulants or depressants, both of which alter brain chemistry, yet this is a time when the brain is trying to construct the neural and cognitive pathways needed for reading and reading comprehension. As a health care provider, I see children from low-income families, as young as four and five years old, who have been diagnosed or treated for ADD/ADHD because they were considered hyperactive. One has to wonder what effect these medications, which are not recommended for children under the age of six, are having on the developing brain. OSAS in children mimics asthma and ADD/ADHD and causes conductive hearing loss and musculoskeletal dysfunction of the head and neck, thus the early differential diagnosis and treatment of OSAS is critical for young children.

To improve the performance of children in reading and reading comprehension, education reform must focus on the preschool, when the growth and development of the brain is most sensitive. How well the child hears the sounds and sees the letters and how the brain assimilates the information in these early years form the foundation for future academic growth and development. Early assessment and identification of children who are neurologically impaired due to OSAS during their preschool years will allow educators to introduce interventions, such as phonemic awareness, with a greater level of success.

Chapter 6

Summary

In *The Mis-Education of the Negro*, Carter G. Woodson (1933) painted a vivid picture of the difficulties that the descendants of slaves encountered in their efforts to obtain an education. Seventy-five years later, much has changed and much has remained the same. The challenges that descendants of slaves face in the areas of health care, education, politics, economics, and social admittance have not diminished, and in some instances they have been exacerbated by the programs and incentives designed to address these issues. In 1998, the Committee on the Prevention of Reading Difficulties in Young Children concluded a project supported by the National Academy of Sciences and the U.S. Department of Education. The published report (Snow, Burns, and Griffin 1998) is a 432-page document that summarizes scientific and education advances as grounds for methods to prevent reading difficulties in children. In identifying the predictors of success and failure in reading, the committee focused on risk factors, including children who had weak language and literacy skills at the outset of schooling. In *Why?* we have identified compromising medical conditions, specifically OSAS, that have a tremendous impact on the development of reading skills in children. OSAS occurs in all populations of children; however, it is the prevalence of OSAS in African American children that skews the reported academic performance levels of these children when compared to their peers.

It would be rhetorical and superfluous for this author to continue to expound on the socioeconomic plight of the African American student; we have touched on the major points of the cause-and-effect relationship between slavery and other social wrongs, on the one hand, and academic success, on the other. We began our inquiry into why African American children cannot read by taking an in-depth look at the tree rather than the forest of data and statistical information. The focal point of the educational process, after all, is the individual child who sits on the front row of Ms. Jones' first-grade class. It is the child who has or has not developed the cognitive skills necessary to navigate the labyrinth of the educational process. We should applaud the national, state, and local offices of education that are making that quantum leap in their understanding and placing more emphasis on early childhood development, particularly those years before the onset of formal education.

Schools are not social service agencies. But they have a responsibility to understand and nurture the real abilities of the individual child, rather than have a preconceived notion of the child's abilities based on the child's race or socioeconomic status. As we have seen, every child, with few exceptions, is born with the genetic capacity and potential to succeed in school and in life. Far too many children are labeled "at risk" by educational and social sorting paradigms in which some students receive high-expectation instruction while the rest are relegated to lower-quality instruction and lower-quality futures. The mandates of No Child Left Behind encourage school systems to "teach to the middle" and develop curriculums that focus on those children who will meet the criteria for showing "annual yearly progress," the bench mark that allows them to keep their federal funding.

Meet Iesha Berry, a tall slender girl of twelve, poised and confident. Her eyes look like large telescopes searching the horizon. Her skin is dark and velvety smooth, typical of African heritage. Her mother's income is less than five thousand dollars per year, and she has no formal education. There is no television in the home and very few personal items. By today's standards, she is considered poor, underprivileged, and at risk. Iesha had no access to Head Start, Sesame Street, or the plethora of social programs designed to assist the low-income child at risk, yet she speaks with a silky smooth voice of amazing clarity and diction that belies her age and circumstances. She attends the Oxford Boarding School in the Village of Konongo in western Ghana, a school that has no windows, doors, or any of the 21st century teaching tools found in classrooms across America. She speaks fluent English, French, and Twi, her native language, and displays the potential for academic growth and development that is paralleled, but often not encouraged, in her American counterparts. The most compelling fact is that Iesha and her American counterparts were born with the same neural framework and the same potential for academic excellence and life success.

Schools are not health care providers. But preschool and day-care providers have the opportunity to assist parents in identifying children who are hyperactive and struggling with the basic cognitive skills, such as sounds, letters, and number recognition. Parents and preschool educators need to know that the signs and symptoms of sleep-related breathing disorders are mouth breathing, snoring at nap time, hyperactivity, lack of focus and attention, hearing difficulties, and poor retention of information. It is the identification of the child with chronic colds or asthmatic symptoms, dark circles under the eyes and who has difficulty with some sounds and words. They should also know that snoring at nap time and not responding to verbal instructions unless spoken to face to face are signs and symptoms of obstructive sleep apnea syndrome. These providers can encourage parents to have their child examined by their primary care physician, because they understand the importance of these early years of growth and development.

During the discussion period following a presentation for Otolaryngologist interns, I was asked if there is a genetic basis for the prevalence of OSAS, and the accompanying poor academic performance in African Americans children. The answer is emphatically no. The impressive achievements of African Americans as inventors, scientists, educators, artists, and numerous other disciplines clearly dispel this notion. There are genetic factors in any ethnic population that could contribute to sub-par academic growth and development. It is the ever-present social, environmental, and health disparities, however, that are the causative agents for poor academic performance among African American children. The cycle of illiteracy, poverty, and social immobility that exists will only be broken if these children are not stigmatized before they exit their mothers' wombs.

Medical science has provided educators with an understanding of the biological factors that determine the cognitive preparedness of the child, and it is the obligation of educators to develop instructional modalities that apply this knowledge. Educators must not stigmatize African American children based on a preconceived evaluation of their social status. Yes, there are cultural differences, just as there are differences with children of many different nationalities in our society.

African American parents must understand their level of responsibility for the quality of health care and education of their children. They must become a part of the process by providing environments that are synergetic with the efforts of educators. Education begins at home, and it is in the home that parents must understand and recognize the child's developmental timetable, not only milestones like the day the baby takes his or her first steps but also the daily behaviors, such as whether the child snores, sleeps restlessly, or has a constant cold.

Health care providers must be more diligent in their evaluation process. Primary care and Emergency Room physicians who see the same child over and over again, presenting with the same chronic or acute breathing conditions, must see beyond the obvious. They must go beyond the restricted parameters of health care systems and treat the conditions, not merely the symptoms. The "ounce of prevention is worth a pound of cure" philosophy must become the standard of care, regardless of the socioeconomic status of the patient. Disparity is truly an appalling word, for due to disparity, many children are truly in despair for the lack of the health care they deserve. The neurological health and development of all children during the preschool years should be a focal point of reforms in education and health care. The early differential diagnosis and treatment of OSAS and other sleep disordered breathing conditions could forever change the landscape of the health care delivery system. The clinical manifestations of OSAS mimic those of asthma, bronchitis, and many other upper-respiratory conditions. Health care professionals are diagnosing asthma in epidemic numbers, even in the presence of OSAS symptoms such as snoring. The Pediatric Society guidelines are specific for children who snore and stop breathing during sleep: if a child's medical history includes snoring or pauses in breathing during sleep, then the guidelines should be treated as a standard of care and not a discretionary protocol. The hyperactive behavior associated with ADD is often a symptom of an underlying SDB. African American children, males in particular, constitute an inordinate and unacceptable percentage of the children diagnosed and treated as ADD and classified as "special," and "at risk," and who perform below proficiency in the academic environment. These percentages belie the true capabilities and potential of these children.

The Answer

African American children who struggle with reading and reading comprehension do so because they fail to completely develop the neurological system for *memory* between the ages of two and five. The thread that connects African American children to social, economic, and educational disparities is this deficiency in reading. We know *why* children have difficulty learning to read, and now we must focus our efforts and resources to begin the process of breaking the cycle of poverty and poor education, upon which the inability to read is founded.

Parents, health care providers and educators are stakeholders in a society that prioritizes incarceration over education, healthcare, and child development.   As a society, we must have the courage to approach the future by facing up to the past and the realities of the present. Parents must embrace the responsibility of providing for their children. Healthcare providers must see beyond the observable and utilize diagnostic and treatment modalities that address the causes rather than the symptoms, no matter what the price.

For education, race and the social economic status of children can no longer serve as bench marks for the assessment of the "at risk" child. Educators must develop and institute programs and curriculums that understand why children cannot read, and place emphasis on developing this skill based on the plasticity of the brain.

If the future of our society to be different the present must be disturbed. Children are our future and the mind is a terrible thing to waste.

THE AUTHOR

Dr. Philip W. Cooper, Jr. currently resides and workes in Savannah, Georgia. He is a graduate of Meharry Medical College – School of Dentistry and Co-Founder and Chief Investigator for Smiles Are Meaningful, Inc., a research organization whose focus is the impact of Sleep Apnea on growth and development in African American Children. Dr. Cooper taught in the public schools of North Carolina, and at Armstrong State College, now Armstrong Atlantic State University, in Savannah, Georgia. He has presented at the National Medical Association, Georgia Dental Society, The Georgia Association of Educators, Chatham Association of Educators, and Parent University. He has conducted seminars for Pre-K programs and community groups on the subject of SLEEP *APNEA AND COGNIGITVE DEVELOPMENT.*

Professionally, Dr. Cooper is a member of the National Dental Association, International Association for Orthodontics, American Association for Functional Orthodontics, Mid American Orthodontic Society, Academy of Sleep Dentistry, National Black Child Development Institute, and a number of other health and education focused organizations.

Dr. Cooper is a member and volunteer on the Medical Team for the Goodness and Mercy Foundation – *Hands Across Africa,* and has served on multiple missions to Ghana and Nigeria, Africa.

Dr. Cooper is committed to helping youth develop to their greatest potential, as is evidenced by his membership on the boards of the Goodness and Mercy Foundation, West Broad Street Y.M.C.A., and the Greenbriar Children's Center.

TODAY IS A GOOD DAY
A BETTER DAY THAN YESTERDAY
AND TOMORROW
WILL BE A BETTER DAY THAN TODAY

P. W. COOPER, JR.

Letters from Parents

The following are samples of letters from parents whose children were diagnosed and treated for obstructive sleep apnea syndrome.

My son Jerell was having difficulty in school with his behavior and staying on task. I was always being called to the school because of his bad behavior. Dr. Cooper suggested he be seen by a specialist because he snored at night and was being considered hyperactive. He was diagnosed with sleep apnea and had his adenoids and tonsils removed. After the surgery, he continued to have behavior problems, but not as often. At one point, he was evaluated by the school's SSI to decide if he needed counseling or medication to control his behavior. After completing the academic testing, he scored so well it was determined that he was not being challenged in school and was acting out because he was bored. Today he stills has periods of poor behavior but is excelling in school. I often wonder if Jerell had been placed on medicine if he would still have the same problems or worse.

T. B.

From Jamal's mother:

> I brought my 4 year old son to you about 10 months ago. I was concerned about him being a mouth breather and snoring whenever he was sleep; also he was not talking much because of his stuttering. When he would speak, I would have to ask him numerously to repeat himself. Most time I pretended to understand what he was saying or understood his question. I did not want him to feel self-conscious about himself. He attended a pre-K program at a public school that tried to correct his speech and teach him the basic numbers and alphabet.
>
> When the teacher was informed that he would be going to a magnet kindergarten class that put emphasis on advanced math and reading, she told me that my child would not succeed in that class because he would not be able to keep up. After you examined him, you suggested that he have his adenoids and tonsils removed because he was not getting enough oxygen. We took him back to his pediatrician and met with some resistance about removing his adenoids and tonsils, even after repeated visits with colds and ear infections. With reluctance he did give us a referral to see an eye, ear, and nose physician. The doctor examined him and was in total agreement with you and the surgery was scheduled. It has been 8 months now and my son is like a new child. He talks constantly, not only keeping up with his classmates, but doing extremely well in school. He sleeps better now and his stuttering is not as noticeable. This is an update on his progress and to say Thank You for helping us get to the bottom of the problem and not prescribing penicillin to fix it.
>
> Thank you,
>
> J. C.

From Raashawyn's mother:

> Raashawyn was a typical child. For seven years raised by his grandmother. He attended the first three years of his schooling at Largo Tibet Elementary School, Savannah, Georgia. During pre-K through second grade there was no complaint about his work or behavior in school.
>
> When he enters the third grade, his third grade teaches made constant calls at home telling us that he is not paying attention or he is not staying in his desk. So one dreary day I took off from work, went to school with Raashawyn. Raashawyn was not out of his desk, just staring into space and not paying attention. So within two days, I went back to school to see what Raashawyn was doing. He was doing he same thing, just staring into space. Spoke with his teacher, with 34 students in his class; she was telling me that your son needs to go on Ritalin. I told her, I do not believe in psychotropic medication for a child. At that time I never heard of the drug.
>
> My husband and I decided to go take Raashawyn to his doctor to see if he can do anything about his attention focus problem. After extensive research about his attention focus problem, I noticed that he was not hyper at home, neither at school, so we narrowed it down to an attention focus problem.
>
> After talking with his doctor, he states that he needs to see a psychologist first, then based on his recommendation he would prescribe Raashawyn medication or not. At this time, everyone was pushing the psychotic medication down my throat. I made an appointment with a psychiatrist doctor. They did a series of studies. I remember the doctor telling me that Raashawyn definitely has attention span dysfunction. His brain was compared to a tube. If the tube is broken into two pieces … such as a fragment of parts, the output is not

being received to his brain. They had a medication that if he takes 10 mg twice a day, it would last all day in order for Raashawyn to make it through school and come home to do homework. For two hours, my husband and I question this doctor thoroughly about this medication. When it winds up the conclusion, to them it was the medicine of choice for school age children.

After talking with that doctor, we had to fight this decision for the next three months. Then finally we came to the conclusion that we will try the medication five days a week.

Then finally one morning I was dressing to go to work, I saw a special on WSAV on Ritalin. Dr. Philip Cooper was on the special stating when is it enough to get your child off Ritalin. His take is that most of the problems are that the child isn't sleeping. His tonsils and adenoids need to come out. I thought about this and did some research on this. Raashawyn did have a bad snoring problem and always slept badly. So finally I went to an ear nose and throat doctor at Memorial Medical Center. He states that it is a simple procedure to remove his tonsils and adenoids.

We schedule Raashawyn for surgery. After removal of his tonsils and adenoids, he no longer snores, not tired when he gets up, he is not restless at night, and mostly he is an A and B student in school. But most of all, he does not use the psychotropic medication for his attention deficit problem.

Mom

We must do this in memory of the dark souls whose weary,
Broken bodies endure the unimaginable.
We must do this on behalf of our children whose thirsty
Spirits clutch for the keys to a future.
This is a struggle that we cannot lose, for in the very making
Of it we will discover, if nothing else, ourselves.

Randall Robinson, *The Debt*

References and Bibliography

Adams, F. 1998. *The Asthma Sourcebook*, 2nd ed. Chicago: NTC Contemporary Publishing.

Adams, R. 2001. *Sideshow U.S.A.: Freaks and the American cultural imagination.* Chicago: University of Chicago Press.

Ansalone, G. 2001. Schooling, tracking, and inequality. *Journal of Children and Poverty* 7 (1): 33–47.

Anyon, J. 1980. Social class and the hidden curriculum. *Journal of Education* 162:67–92.

Artiles, A. J., R. Rueda, J. J. Salazar, and I. Higareda. 2002. English-language learner representation in special education in California urban school districts. In *Racial inequality in special education*, ed. D. J. Losen and G. Orfield, 117–36. Cambridge, MA: Harvard Education Press(

Asthma and Allergy Foundation, **Disparities in Asthma Care** 2003.

The Atlanta Daily World. 1954. Nation's top Negro educators issue important release. November 4.

The Atlanta Journal and Constitution. 1995. All of our children are 'gifted.' June 12.

Barnes, C., G. Mercer, and T. Shakespeare. 1999. *Exploring disability: A sociological introduction.* Malden, MA: Polity.

Bell, Jr., D. A. 1992. *Faces at the bottom of the bell: The permanence of racism.* New York: Basic Books.

———. 1995. Brown v. Board of Education and the interest convergence dilemma. In *Critical race theory: The key writings that formed the movement*, ed. K. Crenshaw, N. Gotanda, G. Peller, and K. Thomas, 20–28. New York: New Press.

Belluck, P. 1996. A plan to revamp special education. *The New York Times*. November 26.

Birney, A. J., and A. M. Hall. 1981. *Children's language disabilities*. SHU Project on Learning and Language. Report No. 10-5432. Washington, D.C.: National Education Association.

Bomer, R., and Bomer, K. 2001. *For a better world: Reading and writing for social action*. Portsmouth, NH: Heinemann.

Bomer, R., J. E. Dworin, L. May, and P. Seminson. 2008. Miseducating teachers about the poor: A critical analysis of Ruby Payne's claims about poverty. *Teachers College Record* 110 (1): 105–15.

Bourgois, P. 1995. *In search of respect: Selling crack in El Barrio*. New York: Cambridge University Press.

Brendan, M. 2005. Funds of knowledge and team ethnography: Reciprocal approaches. In *Funds of knowledge: Theorizing practices in households, communities, and classrooms*, ed. N. Gonzales, L. Moll, and C. Amanti, 199–212. Mahwah, NJ: Erlbaum.

Brown v. Board of Education. 1955. 349 United States Reports 294.

Byrd, J. A. 1989. Cultural patterns of identity definition. *Anthropology Research Quarterly* 9:321–79.

Capdevila, O. S., V. M. Crabtree, L. Kheirandish-Gozal, and D. Gozal. 2008. **Increased morning brain natriuretic peptide levels in children with nocturnal enuresis and sleep- disordered breathing: A community-based study.** *Pediatrics* 121 (5): e1208–14.

Carno, M.-A., E. Ellis, E. Anson, R. Kraus, J. Black, R. Short, and H. V. Connolly. 2008. **Symptoms of sleep apnea and polysomnography as predictors of poor quality of life in overweight children and adolescents.** *Journal of Pediatric Psychology* 33 (3): 269–78.

Carrier, J. 1986. *Learning disability: Social class and the construction of inequality in American education*. New York: Greenwood Press.

Center for Outcome Analysis. The ISSIS database. Unpublished report. Rosemont, PA.

Charleston, W. V. 1955. [Letter to the editor.] *Southern School News*. June.

Chervin, R., K. H. Archbold, J. E. Dillon, P. Panahi, K. J. Pituch, R. E. Dahl, and C. Guilleminault. 2002. Inattention, hyperactivity, and symptoms of sleep disordered breathing. *Pediatrics* 109 (3): 449–56.

Chervin, R. D., K. H. Archbold, P. Panahi, and K. J. Pituch. 2001. Sleep problems seldom addresses at two general pediatric clinics. *Pediatrics* 107 (6): 1375–80.

Chervin R. D., D. F. Clarke, J. L. Huffman, E. Szymanski, D. L. Ruzicka, V. Miller, A. L. Nettles, M. R. Sowers, and B. J. Giordani. 2003. School performance, race and other correlates of sleep disordered breathing in children. *Sleep Medicine* 4 (1): 21–27.

Glaze, D. M. Bautista, K. Evankovich, M.L. Chapieski, E. Friedman, M.G. Stewart, M. Wise, M. Sockroder, amd O.Smith. 2002 Obstructive sleep apnea in children: Impact on congitin, behavior and quality of life, Boca raton, flordia. Press release Annual Meting of the American Society of Pediatric otolaryngology – 13 May.

Compton-Lilly, C. 2003. *Reading families: The literate lives of urban children.* New York: Teachers College Press.

Conroy, J. W. 1999. Connecticut's special education labeling and displacement practices: Analysis of Connor, M. H., and Boskin, J. (2001). Overrepresentation of bilingual and poor children in special education classes. *Journal of Children and Poverty* 7:23–32.

Cookson, P. W. 1994. *School choice: The struggle for the soul of American education.* New Haven, CT: Yale University Press.

Deschenes, S., L. Cuban, and D. Tyack. 2001. Mismatch: Historical perspectives on schools and students who don't fit them. *Teachers College Record* 103 (4): 525–47.

Ferri, B. A. and D. J. Connor. 2004. Special education and the subverting of Brown. *The Journal of Gender, Race, and Justice* 8 (1): 57–74.

2005. Tools of exclusion: Race, disability, and (re)segregated education. *Teachers College Record* 107 (3): 453–74.

Fierros, E. G., and J. W. Conroy. 2002. Double jeopardy: An exploration of restrictiveness and race in special education. In *Racial inequity in special education,* ed. D. J. Losen and G. Orfield, 39–70. Cambridge, MA: Harvard Education Press.

Fleischer, D. Z., and F. Zames. 2001. *The disabilities rights movement: From charity to confrontation.* Philadelphia: Temple University Press.

Foucault, M. 1990. *The history of sexuality: An introduction,* vol. 1. New York: Vintage.

Franklin, B. M. 1987. The first crusade for learning disabilities: The movement for the education of backward children. In *The foundations of the school subjects,* ed. T. Popkewitz, 190–209. London: Falmer.

Gozal, D. 1998. Sleep-disordered breathing and school performance in children. *Pediatrics* 102 (3): 616–20.

Gartner, A., and D. K. Lipsky. 1987. Beyond special education: toward a quality system for all students. *Harvard Education Review* 57 (4): 367–95.

Gee, J. 1990. *Social linguistics and literacies.* London: The Falmer Press.

Giddens, A. 1973. *The class structure of the advanced societies.* New York: Harper & Row.

Gilbert, D. 2003. *The American class structure in an age of growing inequality.* Belmont, CA: Wadsworth/Thompson Learning.

Giordani, B. and R. D. Chervin. 2008. **Sleep-disordered breathing and neurobehavioral outcomes: In search of clear markers for children at risk.** *Journal of the American Medical Association* 299 (17): 2078–80.

Gladwell, M. 2002. *The tipping point.* New York: Little Brown and Company.

Gonzáles, N., L. Moll, and C. Amanti, eds. 2005. *Funds of knowledge: Theorizing practices in households, communities, and classrooms.* Mahwah, NJ: Erlbaum.

Goodman, W. 1994. Disabled: Public or special school? *The New York Times.* September 7.

Gould, S. J. 1996. *The mismeasure of man.* New York: W. W. Norton.

Guskey, T. R., and M. Huberman, eds. 1995. *Professional development in education.* New York: Teachers College Press.

Hahn, H. 1997. New trends in disability studies: Implications for educational policy. In *Inclusion and school reform: Transforming America's classrooms*, ed. D. K. Lipsky and A. Gartner, 315–28. Baltimore: Brookes.

Halbower, A. C., S. L. Ishman, and B. M. McGinley. 2007. **Childhood obstructive sleep-disordered breathing: A clinical update and discussion of technological innovations and challenges.** *Chest* 132 (6): 2030–41.

Harry, B. 1992. Cultural diversity, families, and the special education system: communication and empowerment. Unpublished manuscript.

Head, L., A. Head, M. Hall, and K. Hall. 1996. Fairfax's exclusive public schools. *The Washington Post*, October 13.

Henry, G. T., L. W. Henderson, and B. D. Ponder. 2004. *Ready or not: A snapshot of children entering kindergarten in Georgia*. Atlanta: Georgia State University, Andrew Young School of Policy Studies.

Hopkins-Golightly, T., S. Raz, and C. J. Sander. 2003. Influence of slight to moderate risk for birth hypoxia on acquisition of cognitive and language function in the preterm infant: A cross-sectional comparison with preterm-birth controls. *Neuropsychology* 17 (1): 3–13.

Hurtado, M. P., E. K. Swift, J. M. Corrigon, eds. 2001. *Envisioning the National Health Care Quality Report*. Institute of Medicine, Committee on the National Quality Report on Health Care Delivery. Washington, DC. National Academies Press.

Imparato, A. J. 2001. Aid disabled students. *The New York Times*. January 28.

Individuals with Disabilities Education Act (IDEA) of 1990. PL 101-476, 20 U.S.C.

Institute of Medicine. 2003. *Unequal treatment: Confronting racial and ethnic disparities in health care*. Washington, DC: National Academies Press.

Ireys, H., S. Shulman, and S. Peterson. 2006. *Prescription drug cost for children with special health care needs*. Update 2. Mathematica Policy Research. http://www.mathematica-mpr.com/Publications/MasterList.aspx.

Jacobson, L. 1994. Disabled kids moving into regular classrooms. 'Inclusion' is on, but critics call it unfair. *The Atlanta Journal and Constitution.* May 9.

Karagiannis, A. 2000. Soft disability in schools: Assisting or confining at risk children and youth? *Journal of Educational Thought* 34 (2): 113–34.

Kastens, T. Y. 1995. My children have a civil right to learn. *The Washington Post.* January 4.

Kauffman, J. M., and D. P. Hallahan, eds. 1995. *The illusion of full inclusion: A comprehensive critique of a current special education bandwagon.* Austin, TX: Pro-Ed.

LeGault, M. 2006. *Th!nk.* New York: Threshold Editions.

Leung, L. C. K., D. K. Ng, M. W. Lau, C. Chan, K. Kwok, P. Chow, and J. M.Y. Cheung. 2006. **Twenty-four-hour ambulatory BP in snoring children with obstructive sleep apnea syndrome.** *Chest* 130 (4): 1009–17.

Levitt, S. and S. Dubner, 2005. *Freakonomics.* New York: Harper Collins Publications Inc.

Linton, S. 1998. *Claiming Disability.* New York: New York University Press.

Losen, D. J., and G. Orfield, eds. 2002. *Racial inequality in special education.* Cambridge, MA: Harvard Education Press

Lumeng, J. C., and R. D. Chervin. 2008. **Epidemiology of pediatric obstructive sleep apnea.** *Proceedings of the American Thoracic Society* 5 (2): 242–52.

Lyon, G. R. 1998. *Overview of reading and literacy initiatives.* Statement to the Committee on Labor and Human Resources, April 28.

McMahon, E. 2002. Mainstreaming Children. *The New York Times.* May 1.

Mercado, C. I. 2005. Reflections on the study of households in New York City and Long Island: A different route, a common destination. In *Funds of knowledge: Theorizing practices in households, communities, and classrooms,* ed. N. Gonzales, L. Moll, and C. Amanti, 233–55. Mahwah, NJ: Erlbaum.

Mickelson, R. A. 2001. Subverting Swann: First and second-generation segregation in the Charlotte-Mecklenburg schools. *American Educational Research Journal* 38 (2): 215–52.

Mitchell, R. B., J. Kelly, E. Call, and N. Yao. 2004. Quality of life after adenotonsillectomy for obstructive sleep apnea in children. *Archives of Otolaryngology—Head and Neck Surgery* 130:190–94.

Morgan, D. 1980. Blacks, whites, critical of Cleveland's desegregation effort. *The Washington Post.* July 28.

Muzumdar, H., and R. Arens. 2008. **Diagnostic issues in pediatric obstructive sleep apnea.** *Proceedings of the American Thoracic Society* 5 (2): 263–73.

The New York Times. 1955. South reacts quietly to high court ruling. June 1.

No Child Left Behind Act of 2001. 2002. Pub. L. No. 107–110.

Nord, M., M. Andrews, S. Carlson. 2006. Household food security in the United States, 2005. Washington, DC: United States Department of Agriculture. http://www.ers.usda.gov/publications/err29/.

Osei-Kofi, N. 2005. Pathologizing the poor: A framework for understanding Ruby Payne's work. *Equity and Excellence* 38 (4): 367–75.

Pajares, M. F. 1992. Teachers' beliefs and educational research: Cleaning up a messy construct. *Review of Educational Research* 62 (3): 307–32.

Patterson, J. T. 2000. *America's struggle against poverty in the twentieth century.* Cambridge, MA: Harvard University Press.

Payne, R. K. 2005. *A Framework for understanding poverty.* Highland, TX: Aha! Process.

Public Schools Excellence Act. 1999. S 7, 106th Cong., 2nd sess. § 301–303.

Redline, S., P. V. Tishler, M. G. Hans, T. D. Tosteson, K. P. Strohl, and K. Spry. 1997. Racial differences in sleep disordered breathing in African Americans and Caucasians. *American Journal of Respiratory and Critical Care Medicine* 155 (1): 186–92.

Restak, R. 2002. *The secret life of the brain.* The Dana Press and the Joseph Henry Press.

Revell, P. 2001. Education: On or out? Who is special? *The Guardian* (London). November 13.

Robinson, R. 2000. *The debt: What America owes to blacks.* Chicago: The Penguin Group.

Ruppmann, J. 1991. Where disabled do best. *The Washington Post.* November 7.

Samad, A. A. 2005. *50 years after Brown: The state of black equality in America.* Los Angeles: Kabili Press.

Sleeter, C. E. 1987. Why is there learning disabilities? A critical analysis of the birth of the field with its social context. In *The foundations of the school subjects,* ed. T. S. Popkewitz, 210–37. London: Palmer Press.

Snow, C., M. Burns, and P. Griffin, eds. 1998. *Preventing reading difficulties in young children.* Washington, DC: National Research Council.

Stepanski, E., A. Zayyad, C. Nigro, M. Lopata, and R. Bansner. 1999. Sleep-disordered breathing in a predominantly African-American pediatric population. *Journal of Sleep Research* 8 (1): 65–70.

Strausberg, C. 1992. Disabled kids' status questioned. *The Chicago Defender.* May 27.

Taylor, D., and C. Dorsey-Gaines. 1988. *Growing up literate: Learning from inner-city families.* Portsmouth, NH: Heinemann.

U.S. Department of Education, Institute of Education Sciences, National Center for Education Statistics. *The Nation's Report Card, Reading (2001 – 2006).*

U.S. Department of Education. 2000. *Elementary and secondary school civil rights compliance report: Projected values for the nation and individual states—1998.* Washington, DC: U.S. Government Printing Office.

U.S. Department of Health and Human Services. 2002. *Protecting the health of minority communities. Fact Sheet,* September 24.

Weis, L. 1988. *Class, race, and gender in American education.* Albany, NY: State University of New York Press.

Weis, L., and M. Fine, eds. 1993. *Beyond silenced voices: Class, race, and gender in United States schools.* Albany, NY: State University of New York Press.

West, C. 2004. *Democracy matters, winning the fight against imperialism.* New York: Penguin.

Wharton, J. 2000. Make the school fit the child: Opinion. *The Times Educational Supplement.* March 3.

Woodson, C.G. 1933. The mis-education of the Negro.

Young, T., P. E. Peppard, and D. J. Gottlieb. 2002. Epidemiology of obstructive sleep apnea: A population health perspective. *Journal of Respiratory and Critical Care Medicine* 165 (9): 1217–39.

Printed in the United States
135900LV00004B/6/P